Comparing Countries

Festivals and Celebrations

Compara países

Festivales y celebraciones

translated into Spanish by Ana Cristina Llompart Lucas

Sabrina Crewe

CRABTREE PUBLISHING COMPANY
WWW.CRABTREEBOOKS.COM

CRABTREE
PUBLISHING COMPANY
WWW.CRABTREEBOOKS.COM

Author: Sabrina Crewe

Editorial director: Kathy Middleton

Designer: Keith Williams

Illustrator: Stefan Chabluk

Translator: Ana Cristina Llompart Lucas

Proofreader: Melissa Boyce

Production coordinator and prepress: Ken Wright

Print coordinator: Katherine Berti

The publisher would like to thank the following for permission to reproduce their pictures: Debbie Aird Photography/Shutterstock 14; Steve Allen/Shutterstock 20; Anitasstudio/Shutterstock front cover (top); Stanislav Beloglazov/Shutterstock front cover (bottom), title page, 8; Paula Bronstein/Getty Images 4; ChameleonsEye/Shutterstock 10; Kobby Dagan/Shutterstock 24; Ian Forsyth/Getty Images 23; Frankris/Shutterstock 18; Kevin Frayer/Getty Images 21; JoJan 28; Teresa Kasprzycka/Shutterstock 16; Kai Keisuke/Shutterstock 29; Patryk Kosmider/Shutterstock 13; Janali Laghari/Pacific Press/Alamy Live News 9; Mamasamala 15; Monkey Business Images/Shutterstock 25; Paparazzi by Appointment/Alamy Stock Photo 7; Pixy Nook/Shutterstock 5; REUTERS/Alamy Stock Photo 17; Romakoma/Shutterstock 11; Spanish Ministry of Defence 19; Tooykrub/Shutterstock 26; Krisztina V/Shutterstock 6; Vichailao/Shutterstock 22; Leanne Vorrias/Shutterstock 12; www.Kremlin.ru 27.

Library and Archives Canada Cataloguing in Publication

Title: Festivals and celebrations = Festivales y celebraciones / Sabrina Crewe.
Other titles: Festivales y celebraciones
Names: Crewe, Sabrina, author. | Llompart, Ana Cristina, translator.
Description: Series statement: Comparing countries = Compara países | Translated into Spanish by Ana Cristina Llompart Lucas. | Previously published: London: Franklin Watts, 2018. | Includes index. | Text in English and Spanish.
Identifiers: Canadiana (print) 20190199164 | Canadiana (ebook) 20190199172 | ISBN 9780778769408 (hardcover) | ISBN 9780778769613 (softcover) | ISBN 9781427124401 (HTML)
Subjects: LCSH: Holidays—Juvenile literature. | LCSH: Festivals—Juvenile literature.
Classification: LCC GT3933 .C74 2020 | DDC j394.26—dc23

Library of Congress Cataloging-in-Publication Data

Names: Crewe, Sabrina, author. | Crewe, Sabrina. Festivals and celebrations. | Crewe, Sabrina. Festivals and celebrations. Spanish. | Chabluk, Stefan, illustrator.
Title: Festivals and celebrations = fiestas y celebraciones / Sabrina Crewe; illustrated by Stefan Chabluk.
Other titles: Fiestas y celebraciones
Description: New York, New York : Crabtree Publishing Company, 2020. | Series: Comparing countries | Includes index.
Identifiers: LCCN 2019043505 (print) | LCCN 2019043506 (ebook) | ISBN 9780778769408 (hardcover) | ISBN 9780778769613 (paperback) | ISBN 9781427124401 (ebook)
Subjects: LCSH: Holidays--Juvenile literature. | Festivals--Juvenile literature.
Classification: LCC GT3933 .C74 2020 (print) | LCC GT3933 (ebook) | DDC 394.26--dc23
LC record available at https://lccn.loc.gov/2019043505
LC ebook record available at https://lccn.loc.gov/2019043506

Crabtree Publishing Company

www.crabtreebooks.com 1-800-387-7650

Published in 2020 by Crabtree Publishing Company

Published in Canada
Crabtree Publishing
616 Welland Avenue
St. Catharines, ON
L2M 5V6

Published in the United States
Crabtree Publishing
PMB 59051
350 Fifth Ave, 59th Floor
New York, NY 10118

Printed in the U.S.A./012020/CG20191115

Contents

Contenido

To read this book in English, follow the orange boxes. To read this book in Spanish, follow the green boxes. Look for the globe on each page. It shows you where each country is in the world and on which continent.

Para leer este libro en inglés, sigue los recuadros en anaranjado. Para leer este libro en español, sigue los recuadros en verde. Busca el globo terráqueo en cada página. Te muestra dónde está ubicado cada país en el mundo y en qué continente.

Celebrate!

A **celebration** is a time to be happy about something. Festivals are celebrations with lots of people. Let's go around the world to see how people celebrate in different countries!

AFGHANISTAN

In Afghanistan, people celebrate the festival of Eid al-Fitr with new clothes. They spend the day with family and friends.

¡Vamos a celebrar!

Una **celebración** es una ocasión para mostrar nuestra alegría por algo. Los festivales son celebraciones con mucha gente. ¡Vamos a recorrer el mundo y ver cómo celebra la gente en distintos países!

AFGANISTÁN

En Afganistán, la gente estrena ropa para celebrar el festival de Eid al-Fitr y pasan el día con la familia y los amigos.

Many festivals happen every year. What is your favorite festival of the year?

Durante el año se celebran muchos festivales. ¿Cuál es tu festival del año favorito?

THAILAND

Festivals can be a time to see something special. A crowd gathers every year to watch hot air balloons take to the sky at a festival in Thailand.

TAILANDIA

En algunos festivales se pueden ver cosas especiales. En un festival de Tailandia, todos los años una enorme multitud se reúne para ver subir por el cielo globos aerostáticos.

Birthdays

Some people celebrate birthdays with parties, presents, and treats. Almost everyone likes birthday cake! Some countries have special ways to celebrate.

Cumpleaños

Algunas personas celebran su cumpleaños con fiestas, regalos y sorpresas. ¡Y a casi todo el mundo le gustan los pasteles de cumpleaños! En algunos países el cumpleaños se celebra de manera especial.

DENMARK

People fly Denmark's flag to celebrate their birthdays. They put flags outside their homes and on their cakes.

DINAMARCA

La gente exhibe la bandera de Dinamarca cuando celebra su cumpleaños. Ponen banderas en la puerta de la casa y en el pastel.

PANAMA

At birthday parties, people hang paper **piñatas** full of treats from a tree. When they break open the piñata, the treats tumble out!

PANAMÁ

En las fiestas de cumpleaños se cuelgan de un árbol **piñatas** de papel llenas de dulces. ¡Al romper la piñata caen todos los dulces!

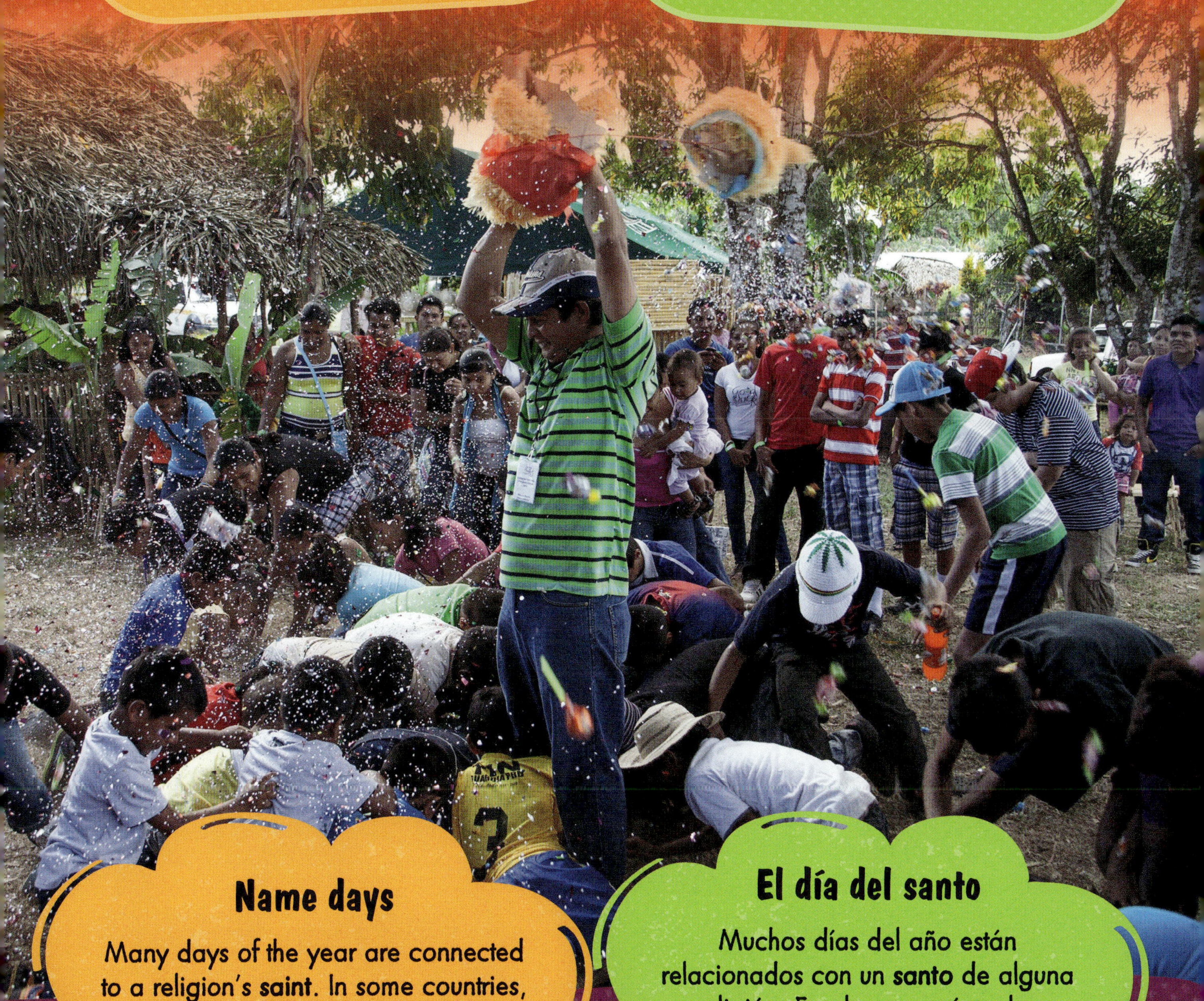

Name days

Many days of the year are connected to a religion's **saint**. In some countries, people celebrate these days if they are named after the saint.

El día del santo

Muchos días del año están relacionados con un **santo** de alguna religión. En algunos países, las personas que llevan el nombre del santo celebran ese día.

Religious festivals

Religious festivals are celebrations of what people believe. People practice different religions around the world.

Festivales religiosos

En los festivales religiosos celebramos nuestras creencias. La gente practica distintas religiones en varias partes del mundo.

INDIA

Most people in India belong to the Hindu religion. At Holi, Hindus throw colored powder on each other to celebrate the **god** Krishna.

INDIA

La mayoría de los habitantes de la India son de religión hindú. En Holi, los hindúes se lanzan polvos de colores unos a otros para celebrar al **dios** Krishna.

PAKISTAN

Eid Milad-un-Nabi is a festival in the Muslim religion. Many Muslims celebrate Eid Milad-un-Nabi with a day of **festivities**.

PAKISTÁN

Eid Milad-un-Nabi es un festival de la religión musulmana. Muchos musulmanes lo celebran con un día de **festividades**.

Festival traditions

Hanukkah and Christmas are religious festivals. They are also a time families celebrate their own **traditions**.

Tradiciones de festivales

Hanukka y Navidad son fiestas religiosas. También son una ocasión para que las familias celebren sus propias **tradiciones**.

UNITED STATES

Hanukkah is the Jewish Festival of Lights. Each night, one candle is used to light another candle. The festival lasts for eight nights.

ESTADOS UNIDOS

Hanukkah es la fiesta judía de las luces. Cada noche, se usa una vela para encender otra. El festival dura ocho noches.

CANADA

People who follow the Christian religion love to **decorate** their trees and houses for Christmas. Snowmen, reindeer, and wreaths are all traditional decorations.

CANADÁ

A la gente que profesa la religión cristiana le encanta **decorar** sus árboles y casas por Navidad. Los muñecos de nieve, los renos y las coronas de Navidad son todas decoraciones tradicionales.

What is a tradition?

A tradition is something that people always do in the same way. Some traditions are just for one family. Others are followed by a lot of people.

¿Qué es una tradición?

Una tradición es algo que la gente siempre hace de la misma manera. Algunas tradiciones son parte solo de una familia, pero otras tradiciones las sigue mucha gente.

Carnivals and parades

A **carnival** is an event where people have fun. There may be games and rides for children. At many carnivals, the crowds join in **parades** and march to the music.

BRAZIL

The world's biggest carnival is in Rio de Janeiro, Brazil. It is famous for its colorful costumes and huge, decorated **floats**.

Carnavales y desfiles

Un **carnaval** es un evento donde la gente se divierte. Puede incluir juegos y atracciones para los niños. En muchos carnavales, la gente participa en **desfiles** y marchan al ritmo de la música.

BRASIL

El mayor carnaval del mundo es el de Río de Janeiro, en Brasil. Es famoso por sus coloridos disfraces y enormes **carrozas** decoradas.

IRELAND

Parades are held in Ireland on St. Patrick's Day in honor of their **patron saint**. People celebrate by putting up flags and wearing green, the traditional color of Ireland.

IRLANDA

En Irlanda se llevan a cabo desfiles en el Día de San Patricio para **honrar** a su **santo patrón** de Irlanda. La gente decora con banderas y viste de verde, el color tradicional de Irlanda.

Weddings

Bodas

Marriage is a time for families to celebrate. Different **cultures** celebrate weddings in different ways.

Las bodas son una ocasión para que la familia celebre. Distintas **culturas** celebran bodas de manera diferente.

SOUTH AFRICA

There is always dancing at Zulu weddings. Family members and friends perform traditional dances.

SUDÁFRICA

En las bodas zulúes siempre hay bailes. Los miembros de la familia y los amigos bailan danzas tradicionales.

What is culture?

Culture is a mix of your beliefs and the way you do things. People can share a country or religion, but they may still belong to different cultures.

¿Qué es la cultura?

La cultura es una mezcla de tus creencias y la manera en la que haces las cosas. La gente puede compartir un país o una religión y aun así pertenecer a culturas diferentes.

INDONESIA

In Indonesia, a Minangkabau bride wears a golden crown called a *suntiang* at her wedding. The **ceremonies** go on for two or three days.

INDONESIA

En Indonesia, una novia minangkabau lleva una corona dorada llamada *suntiang* en su boda. Las **ceremonias** duran dos o tres días.

Festive food

When people have something to celebrate, they like to prepare a **feast**. All around the world, people make special foods for holidays and celebrations.

Comida festiva

Cuando la gente tiene algo que celebrar, le gusta preparar un **festín**. En todo el mundo, la gente prepara comida especial en las celebraciones y los días de fiesta.

POLAND

People in Poland love to cook special meals. Their most important feast is on Christmas Eve. They serve twelve **festive** dishes, including fish, beetroot soup, and fruitcake.

POLONIA

A las personas de Polonia les encanta cocinar comidas especiales. Su festín más importante es en Nochebuena. Sirven doce platos **festivos**, como pescado, sopa de remolacha y pastel de frutos secos.

FRANCE

The French are famous for their food, especially chocolate! The Easter holiday is a time for making traditional chocolate eggs and other shapes.

FRANCIA

Los franceses son famosos por su comida, ¡especialmente el chocolate! Semana Santa es la época de hacer los tradicionales huevos de chocolate y otras figuras.

What food do you eat on special days?

¿Qué comes tú en días especiales?

National days

National days celebrate **nations**, or countries. People **display** their national colors and wear traditional costumes. They show they are proud of their country.

Fiestas nacionales

Las fiestas **nacionales** celebran una **nación**, es decir un país. La gente **hace gala de** los colores de su nación y viste trajes tradicionales. Demuestran que están orgullosos de su país.

UNITED ARAB EMIRATES

On December 2, people in United Arab Emirates celebrate National Day, when seven **emirates** united into one nation. All over the country, people watch parades and carry flags.

EMIRATOS ÁRABES UNIDOS

El 2 de diciembre, el Día Nacional, se celebra la unión de siete **emiratos** en una sola nación. En todo el país, la gente asiste a desfiles y lleva banderas.

SPAIN

Spain's national day is Hispanic Day on October 12. Crowds watch as airplanes perform a daring display in the sky. The red and yellow trails match the colors of Spain's national flag.

ESPAÑA

El día nacional de España es el 12 de octubre, Día de la Hispanidad. La multitud mira cómo los aviones realizan una arriesgada demonstración aérea. Sus estelas de humo rojas y amarillas son como los colores de la bandera nacional española.

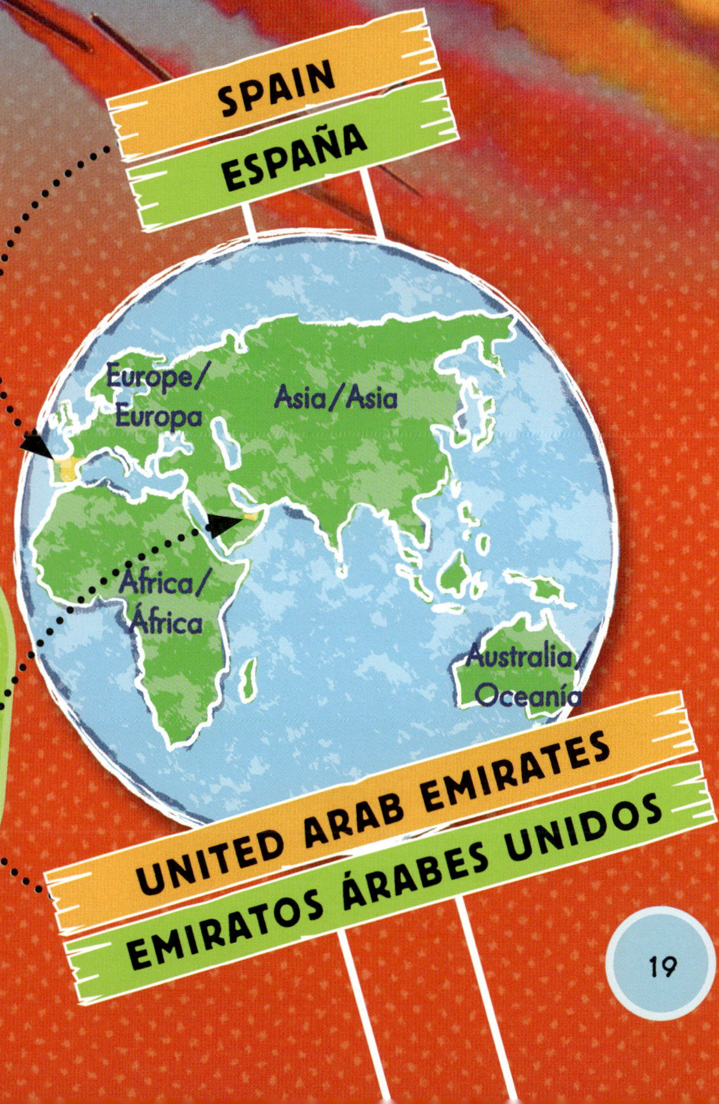

Fireworks!

When people celebrate at night, they love to watch fireworks. Fireworks make lots of noise and create a colorful display.

GREAT BRITAIN

Guy Fawkes Night is on November 5 in Great Britain. People gather around bonfires and set off fireworks. The fireworks remind people that Guy Fawkes plotted to blow up the **government** in 1605.

Danger!

Fireworks are dangerous. Always stand a safe distance away.

¡Fuegos artificiales!

En las celebraciones nocturnas, la gente disfruta viendo fuegos artificiales: hacen mucho ruido y crean un espectáculo de color.

GRAN BRETAÑA

En Gran Bretaña, la noche de Guy Fawkes es el 5 de noviembre. La gente se reúne alrededor de fogatas y lanza fuegos artificiales para recordar que, en 1605, Guy Fawkes conspiró para hacer volar con pólvora al **gobierno**.

¡Peligro!

Los fuegos artificiales son peligrosos. Siempre debes mantenerte alejado y seguro.

CHINA

Chinese New Year is celebrated with dancing dragons, fireworks, and firecrackers. The noisy firecrackers are set off to scare away bad **spirits**.

CHINA

El Año Nuevo Chino se celebra con dragones danzantes, fuegos artificiales y ruidosos cohetes, que se sueltan para espantar con ellos a los malos **espíritus**.

Celebrating seasons

Celebraciones de las estaciones

Some festivals mark the change of the seasons. People celebrate these changes, from cold to warm or from dark to light.

Algunos festivales señalan el cambio de las estaciones. La gente celebra estos cambios, de frío a calor o de oscuridad a luz.

JAPAN

The cherry blossom festival happens in spring in Japan. When the cherry trees blossom, families have picnics under the trees.

JAPÓN

El festival de los cerezos en flor tiene lugar en Japón durante la primavera. Cuando brotan las flores del cerezo, las familias hacen un pícnic bajo los árboles.

SWEDEN

In December, people in Sweden wear white to celebrate St. Lucia, the patron saint of light. Girls wear crowns of candles and boys wear pointed hats.

SUECIA

En diciembre, las personas de Suecia se visten de blanco para la celebración de Santa Lucía, santa patrona de la luz. Las niñas llevan coronas de velas y los niños sombreros de punta.

Harvest festivals

Harvest is the time when farmers gather their crops. Harvest festivals traditionally celebrate having enough food for the months ahead.

Festivales de la cosecha

En la época de la cosecha, los granjeros recogen sus cultivos. Tradicionalmente, los festivales de la cosecha celebran que, durante los próximos meses, habrá suficiente comida.

Ghosts and spirits

Fantasmas y espíritus

Some festivals celebrate the dead and ghosts and spirits. Their traditions come from old beliefs that the dead come back to visit us.

Algunos festivales celebran a los muertos, los fantasmas y los espíritus. Estas tradiciones tienen su origen en antiguas creencias según las cuales los muertos regresaban a visitarnos.

MEXICO

On the Day of the Dead in Mexico, people visit graves to remember their family members who have died. They decorate the graves with skulls and flowers.

MÉXICO

En México, el Día de los Muertos, la gente visita las tumbas de los familiares fallecidos para recordarlos. Decoran las lápidas con calaveras y flores.

UNITED STATES

Hallowe'en is a night for children to dress up as ghosts, witches, and other scary things. In the United States, children go trick-or-treating to collect treats from their neighbors.

ESTADOS UNIDOS

Halloween es una noche para que los niños se disfracen de fantasmas, brujas y otros seres temibles. En los Estados Unidos, los niños van a las casas de sus vecinos para hacerles "truco o trato" y recolectar dulces.

Do you have costumes or other clothes for special occasions?

¿Tienes disfraces u otros trajes para ocasiones especiales?

Remembering the past

Recordamos el pasado

On certain days, people celebrate history. They remember important events or **heroes** from the past. Usually, the whole country celebrates.

En ciertos días, la gente celebra su historia. Recuerdan sucesos importantes o **héroes** del pasado. Normalmente, son celebraciones en todo el país.

AUSTRALIA AND NEW ZEALAND

On Anzac Day, Australians and New Zealanders remember soldiers who died in World War I (1914–1918). People put flowers on memorials and graves.

AUSTRALIA Y NUEVA ZELANDA

El Día de Anzac, los australianos y los neozelandeses recuerdan a los soldados que murieron en la Primera Guerra Mundial (1914–1918). Ponen flores sobre monumentos y tumbas.

RUSSIA

The Victory Day parade on May 9 reminds Russians of the end of World War II (1939–1945). They mark the day with **military marching**.

RUSIA

El desfile del Día de la Victoria, el 9 de mayo, hace que los rusos recuerden el final de la Segunda Guerra Mundial (1939–1945). Señalan ese día con **marchas militares**.

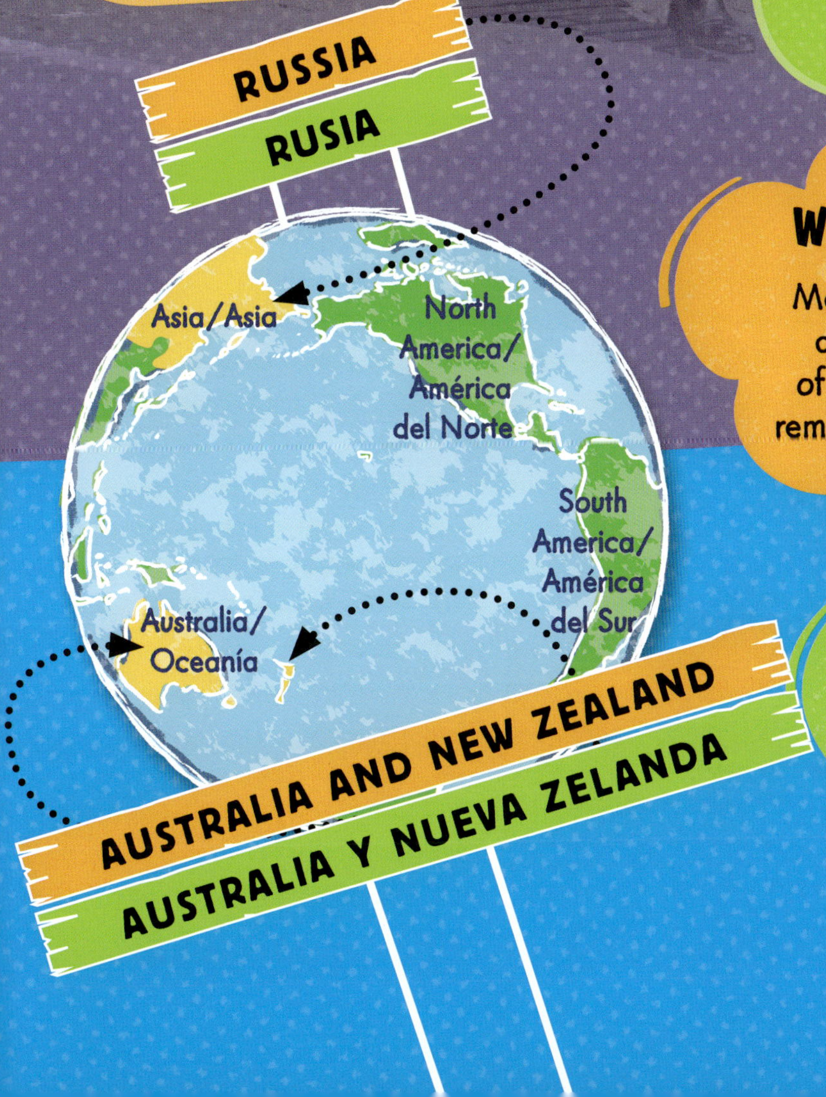

What is a memorial?

Memorials, such as statues, are things that remind us of the past. They help us to remember people and events.

¿Qué es un monumento?

Los monumentos, como las estatuas, son algo que nos hace acordarnos del pasado y nos ayuda a recordar a personas y sucesos.

Children's days

In many countries, children have their own day to show them that they are loved. Children's days also celebrate the future.

TURKEY

The children's festival in Turkey is called Çocuk Bayrami. Children dress up in traditional vests, aprons, and white shirts.

Días del Niño

En muchos países hay un día dedicado solo a los niños; es una manera de mostrarles cariño. El Día del Niño también celebra el futuro.

TURQUÍA

El festival de los niños en Turquía se llama Çocuk Bayrami. Los niños y las niñas llevan chalecos, delantales y camisas blancas tradicionales.

JAPAN

On Children's Day in Japan, families fly fish-shaped flags to honor their children. The fish stand for strength and energy.

JAPÓN

En Japón, el Día del Niño, las familias hacen ondear banderas con forma de pez en honor de sus hijos. El pez representa fuerza y energía.

International Children's Day

International Children's Day is on June 1. It celebrates children all around the world!

Día Internacional del Niño

El Día Internacional del Niño es el 1.º de junio. ¡Celebra a todos los niños del mundo!

Glossary

carnival A festival or celebration with parades, music, food, games, and rides

celebration An enjoyable event to mark a special occasion

ceremony An event marking a special occasion, often with speeches, songs, or prizes

culture A combination of beliefs and customs that belong to a particular group

decorate To make something look attractive

display To show something off

emirate A country or state ruled by a Muslim ruler or chief

feast A large or special meal

festive To do with a festival or something else fun or special

festivities Celebrations that take place at parties, parades, or festivals

floats Flat vehicles decorated for parades

god A powerful spirit or being that has different names and forms depending on people's religion

government The group of leaders that makes decisions and laws for a country

hero A person who is admired for doing brave, difficult, or good things

honor To respect and show admiration for a person or thing

international To do with more than one country or all countries

military To do with soldiers or with any of the armed forces, such as the army or navy

nation A country and the people who live in that country

national To do with a nation. A national flag, for example, is the flag that represents a particular nation.

parade A moving line or crowd of people, often joined by vehicles, floats, and marching bands. Parades happen at carnivals, festivals, and important occasions.

patron saint A very good and holy person in the Christian religion who is believed to protect a particular place, thing, or group of people

piñatas Decorated paper containers full of treats that children break open with a stick

religious To do with spiritual beliefs shared by a group of people, such as Buddhists, Christians, Hindus, and Muslims. Many religions also worship gods and offer people rules and values to live by.

saint Someone chosen and remembered by the Christian church because his or her life was a perfect example of how Christians are supposed to live

spirit The part of a person that is not their physical body. Some people believe this part continues to exist after the body dies.

tradition Something that people always do in the same way and may pass on to younger people in their family or community

Glosario

(carnival) carnaval Festival o celebración con desfiles, música, comida, juegos y atracciones

(celebration) celebración Evento entretenido con el que se señala una ocasión especial

(ceremony) ceremonia Evento que señala una ocasión especial, a menudo con discursos, canciones o premios

(culture) cultura Combinación de creencias y costumbres que son parte de un grupo en particular

(decorate) decorar Hacer que algo se vea hermoso

(display) hacer gala de Enseñar algo de manera especial y con orgullo

(emirate) emirato País o un estado gobernado por un dirigente o jefe musulmán

(feast) festí Comida grande o especial

(festive) festivo Que está relacionado con un festival o algo divertido o especial

(festivities) festividades Celebraciones que tienen lugar durante fiestas, desfiles o festivales

(floats) carrozas Vehículos planos decorados para los desfiles

(god) dios Un espíritu o ser poderoso que tiene diferentes nombres y formas dependiendo de la religión de las personas

(government) gobierno El grupo de líderes que toma decisiones y crea leyes para un país

(hero) héroe Persona que es admirada por haber hecho algo valiente, difícil o por haber realizado actos buenos

(honor) honrar Respetar y mostrar admiración por una persona o un objeto

(international) internacional Algo que tiene que ver con más de un país o con todos los países

(military) militar Algo que tiene que ver con soldados o con cualquiera de las fuerzas armadas, como el ejército o la marina

(nation) nación País y la gente que vive en él

(national) nacional Algo que tiene que ver con una nación. Por ejemplo, la bandera nacional es la bandera que representa a una nación en particular.

(parade) desfile Fila de personas o multitud en movimiento, a menudo acompañada de vehículos, carrozas y bandas de música que marchan. Los desfiles tienen lugar en los carnavales, festivales y otras ocasiones especiales.

(patron saint) santo patrón Persona muy buena y santa de la religión cristiana que se cree que protege un lugar, un objeto o a un grupo de personas en particular

(piñatas) piñatas Envases de papel decorados y rellenos de dulces que los niños rompen con un palo

(religious) religioso Algo que tiene que ver con las creencias espirituales que comparte un grupo de personas, como los budistas, los cristianos, los hindúes y los musulmanes. Muchas religiones también adoran a dioses y ofrecen reglas y valores para que la gente viva de acuerdo a ellos.

(saint) santo Alguien que la iglesia cristiana escoge y recuerda porque su vida fue un ejemplo perfecto de cómo se supone que deben vivir los cristianos

(spirit) espíritu Aquella parte de una persona que no es el cuerpo físico. Algunas personas piensan que el espíritu continúa existiendo después de que el cuerpo muere.

(tradition) tradición Algo que la gente siempre hace de la misma manera y que puede pasar a los miembros más jóvenes de una familia o comunidad

Index

Índice

El índice español no sigue el mismo orden que el inglés.